Introduct

CW00504738

My name is Fraser Hay, founder of Gr(
FREE Group on Facebook and I stay 60 ....s ...u.... of Aberdeen,
and 14 miles past the back of beyond in the highlands of Scotland.

Back in 2003, I and two friends – Stewart and Jeff, raised £150,000
in Angel Funding to create a business based on a membership model
using an online platform. It generated £240,000 in 10 months, but
the IT, programming and development costs ending up costing us
over £200,000. Oh how, things have changed.

Lesson Learned – Moore's Law!! Don't invest all your cash in the platform.

In 2006, I achieved 100 specific goals and generated hundreds of
testimonials on the UK's oldest social network – Ecademy.com. I
wrote my first book "How to Make Money on Ecademy" and had
over 1500 downloads in 2 weeks. I made £10,000 ($15,000) from a
client who I've never met, residing in a country that I've never
visited, which has a language that I can't even speak. Fun times ;)

Lesson Learned – Seek first to understand then to be understood.

In 2008, I set up a platform called The Results Academy, at the time
the entire global financial economy went into meltdown. Ouch, that
was one helluva of an experience. You can read more about it in my
book – "Resilience."

Lesson learned – Timing is everything. 'Nuff said ;)

In 2013, I wrote 10 books about small business marketing and
entrepreneurship in 10 months, and got all 10 to the #1 spot for their

category on Amazon. I also signed up to NING.com, created a community with a view to keeping the numbers quite low so that instead of relying on membership fees, sponsorship or advertising revenue like nearly all other membership sites, I created a lifestyle from my kitchen table creating over 300 videos, over 500 blog articles, and a very powerful, practical 4 step process to help the members make progress with their marketing and business activities.

Lesson learned – Content is King. You need a process – that works.

I then turned my attention to LinkedIn, and generated some positive results, testing, tweaking and trying different approaches, and some of my results included:-

- 250,000 Blog Views to a Post on LinkedIn Pulse
- 400+ Profile Views in 24 hrs.
- 60,000+ views to a single status update
- £7,000 in 7 days following my 3 prong – IPR strategy
- A promotion of my LinkedIn Kindle book got to #1 position for its category in 9 countries
- Got my profile to #2 on Google

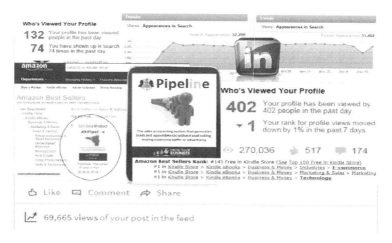

Lesson Learned – Givers gain, takers drain, lurkers simply remain the same.

On March 16th, 2019, I set up a group on Facebook. This book chronicles my launch, content strategy and approach that has enabled me to generate members, leads and sales during my first week. More importantly, it enabled the members to start generating relationships, introductions, referrals, and engagement. It also helped them to raise their profile and some even made money following a very powerful process, ethos and a delightful over-riding principle – "Action Takers Get Rewarded".

The following was achieved in soft launch:-

100 Members – Goal: 28 Days Achieved in 3 Days
Members generating leads, referrals & Sales. Goal: 28 Days Achieved: 5 Days
Turned Focus to Engagement.
1000 Posts, Comments & Reactions – Goal: 28 Days. Achieved in 7 Days
2000 Posts, Comments & Reactions – Goal: 56 Days. Achieved in 14 Days
3700 Posts, Comments & Reactions – Goal: 90 Days. Achieved by Day 22.
Book Written & Published on Amazons – Goal 120 Days. Achieved by Day 23.

Lesson Learned – Lots. I've shared most of them here and even more inside the group ;)

 When you see this symbol throughout the book. Pause & Reflect. Make notes, Answer the Question or Complete the exercise. This will greatly assist you.

Just reading and reflecting on the content of this book will have little effect on the results you generate on Facebook until you convert these "thoughts" into action by applying them. Sorry, but it's true. I can lead a horse to water, but I can't make it drink and on Grow Your Business Club, Action takers get rewarded. In the club, I call Action Takers - HCQPIs – More on that later ;)

Let's make your next 12 months online the best you've ever had. For you just don't know how big it could get…

Fraser J Hay
Founder of Grow Your Business Club
April 07 2019

Copyright Notice & Disclaimer

I also apologise if there are any typos remaining, but my eyesight is improving – thank you.

Your future performance on Facebook is down to you, your attitude, your choices, your behaviours, and your consistent ability to read, relate, assimilate and apply the Facebook marketing tactics I share in the following pages and in my Facebook group – Grow Your Business Club.

I also dedicate this book to my wife Wendy Hay & 5 Kids – The original HCQPIs
(With tattoos to prove it.) ;)

Vicky, Lauren, Wendy, Fraser, Scott, Charlotte, Chloe

Table of Contents

Part One – Social Networking

https://www.haycademy.com

A wee tip of the hat, and a nod – to the first social networking platform I had fun on – Ecademy.com. Respect 😊 I met some amazing people and formed great friendships which continue today and many of them are members in Grow Your Business Club.

Social Networking – Back to the Future

Anyone remember Ecademy.com?

I was quite shy and introverted in these days and still cutting my teeth in this new phenomenon called social networking. Unlike the many running around London and having daily meetings in hotel foyers, private members clubs, the IOD and attending almost daily networking breakfasts, lunches and suppers...

...I connected with folks from all over the globe, helped them where I could, and shared a few beers, Riojas and card tricks with many I encountered

Living 60 miles north of Aberdeen, I even persuaded Thomas Power to come up and meet for a coffee in Aberdeen.

The moral is, you can surprise everyone, **including yourself** (I know I have, living up here 60 miles north of Aberdeen), when you put your mind to it.

If you were a member of Ecademy circa 2006 - 2012, and have fond memories of the pioneering and prospecting days of old, feel free to add a memory or two at the bottom.

Below are 100 things people on Ecademy told me you that couldn't do, which I subsequently went on to achieve.

1. You can't grow your Ecademy network to over 4000 staying 14 miles past the back of beyond

2. You can't generate 400 testimonials on Ecademy in less than 10 years, it takes a long time to build relationships apparently

3. You can't reach the top 100 ranks on Ecademy without attending London Events

4. You can't generate a **59% positive response to an email campaign** to Ecademists (and get record spam complaints too)

5. You can't get Thomas Power to travel 500 miles+ to have a 121 with you. (We found each other in Aberdeen no problem)

6. You can't write a book in **24 hours** (even if it does take 6 mths to edit)

7. You can't get a room of Blackstars to touch their nose and then do a world's first - "dance networking" (course you can)

8. You can't show a fellow Ecademist how to generate **100 referrals in a week** (I did. just ask @Iain Whyte)

9. You can't create an automated self-qualifying lead generation system using Ecademy (it all starts with my profile)

10. You can't get testimonials from Thomas, Penny, Paul, William, Judith **and Glenn** (yup you can - OK Glenn's is a video testimonial)

11. You can't generate over **9500 views to a blog** that's NOT about becoming a Blackstar. (Yup, but you're gonnae have to find it)

12. You can't keep apologising when you cock up, people will get annoyed. (**Best way I think IS to apologise** after you cock up)

13. You can't keep offering excellent diagnostic tools for FREE, you should charge for them. (you're right, Testing is over!)

14. You can generate over **160** comments to a blog unless you're the management

15. You can't generate over 50 testimonials in a single evening - You can if you deliver value.

16. You can't offer **100% of your turnover for the next month to another Ecademist to help them out of a financial hole**.

17. You can't give up your quality time in the evening just to help people in desperate situations. (Why not?)

18. You can't generate **4000** views to an April fool's day blog about Aliens (I did enjoy that one.)

19. You can't have a bigger queue to your speaking slot than the queue to the dragons den slot at the same event (I did.)

20. You can't be a member of Last Thursday, WCP and BS and still be taken seriously and invite Jim Wade and his family out to lunch in Cullen where you live. (Yup 😄;))

21. You can't generate over £5000 from Marketplace ads in less than 24 hours (you won't if you believe no-one reads them)

22. You can't get new members to visit your profile without emailing them a welcome message

23. You can't have both Jim Wade and William Buist's phone numbers on your mobile. Course you can, they're both amazing!

24. You can't get **testimonials from 100 Blackstars** unless you're the management. (Now there's a challenge)

25. You can't have a call to action in your blogs, that's too much like "relentless self-promotion"

26. You can't generate a **2400% ROI for a fellow Ecademist**. (Why not ask Dylan Jones)

27. You can't sell in your autoresponders it's too much like "relentless self-promotion" (so why would you follow up someone??)

28. You can't keep giving valuable advice in your blogs, people will copy it, worse still profit from it

29. You can't crowd dive at a Blackstar Christmas party or dance with members of the same sex

30. You can't make a rap song from a from a blog get 90 comments and generate money for Charity

31. You can't go just making indiscriminate donations to Ecademists charities or fund raising

32. You can't generate testimonials without giving testimonials first (Bollocks.)

33. You can' run a commercial club and a touchy feely spiritual club - that'll send out mixed messages - course you can.

34. You can't write a blog entitled "oggie. oggie. oggie" - No-one

will read it, never mind comment on it. They did 😊;)

35. You can't repeatedly keep wanting to be nice to people who you know stab you in the back and kick you in the nuts

36. You can't ask people for testimonials if they've blagged your IPR for FREE

37. You can't go 28 hours without sleep just to produce work for a client for them not to use it or pay you (nope, never again)

38. You can't get people to sign an NDA for a 1-2-1 (it's just not the Dunn thing to do.)

39. You can't earn **£1000 for an hour's work on behalf of fellow Ecademists**, and them think it's excellent value

40. You can't start up a club on Ecademy and expect to have members from over 31 countries.

41. You can't have an interest in more than one business - you must stay focused

42. You can't use twitter as a serious marketing tool it's for sending messages to your girlfriend!

43. You can't get people to travel from America and turn up a day early for one of your workshops

44. You can't keep that level of energy up - I'll give you 3 months at the most - they said.

45. You can't afford to miss a Blackstar day, (You can't afford to go, and not give value. Really?)

46. You can't say one thing and do another - I know, it's annoying when you see people do it, isn't it

47. You can't just want to help people - no one is that naive what about the money? (Some people are just "wired" differently)

48. You can't socialise with people on Last Thursday if you are a Blackstar - of course you can. Some even became clients.

49. You can't **give someone a blank cheque at a 1-2-1** & ask them to **quantify the value they've just given you** - loved this one - you know who you are 😊;)

50. You can't go to a networking event without an Elevator Pitch, Killer Qualify Question & Free Item of value - but most do

51. You can't speak to 65 Ecademists by phone in a single day. (Why not?)

52. You can't **get a £10,000 sale from an Ecademist you haven't met, in a country you haven't even visited**

53. You can't read a blog about horse sex, then consider staying at the woman's house who wrote it.

54. You can't write a blog and get 2000 views about "10 things to consider when buying a sheep" (worth a try)

55. You can't give out fake winning lottery tickets at a networking event just for a laugh

56. You can't turn a complainee into a customer via Ecademy - those that press that complaint button are a funny lot

57. You can't go giving copies of your book about Ecademy away for FREE after generating 1500 downloads in n 2 weeks.

58. You can't generate **200 referrals in a week completely online**.

59. You can't get a testimonial from Jim Wade he's a cynical old bugger

60. You can't **use the word "tit" in a blog** and not receive a single complaint

61. You can't keep telling people accusing you of spam on Ecademy to start using the same tools Ecademy offer you

62. You can't get **people in a different country to complete a coaching program without a "face-to-face"**

63. You can't phone up an Ecademist feeling lonely in a Singapore hotel, and say "Smile. I read your blog" - tell them it's true <u>Philip Calvert</u> 😊;)

64. You can't **give away your clients and the income stream to other Ecademists to generate cash flow for them**

65. You can't get Ecademists to phone you up and **apologise to you for them being an "arse"** - you can

66. You can't write a book on how to make money on Ecademy if you don't own the website - guess what?

67. You can't **get accommodation in Marble Arch for less than £40 a night** (you can if you're Scottish)

68. You can't get 100,000 marketing questions answered by Ecademists to find out where the real opportunities lie

69. You can't **keep putting other people first, despite your own technical, financial, family and health challenges.**

70. You can't go to appointments having not fully qualified the prospect first. (I know. But some people do.)

71. You can't open up and share details about the way "you feel about your mum", people will laugh. **(Well I cried!)**

72. You can't accept a bet that you'll create 20 videos on YouTube in a week (oh god, not another late night or two that means I'll miss judge Judy or EastEnders)

73. You can't go to a networking event and arrive without business cards - I know but some people do.

74. You can't create a networking audit or networking ROI calculator as there's not a market for it - ?!?!?

75. You can't make an impact, impression or contribute on Ecademy unless you are a Blackstar.

76. You can't get Ecademists to pay £8,000 for a 2 day training course, as there's no money on Ecademy, apparently

77. You can't increase someone's Life Time Value of a Client by 3-400% & give them, 5 new revenue streams. (Why not?)

78. You can't **give advice to someone with a business that's bigger and better than yours - everyone can.**

79. You can't give the same advice to 4 different people in 4 different types of businesses (if they need it, I will)

80. You can't network with 2 glamorous Russian Ladies in the back of a taxi having just left the Tower hotel and decline to do business with them

81. You can't create software to help Ecademists to get an even faster ROI from their membership

82. You can't generate 400 testimonials without meeting them all personally at 121s first?

83. You can't do dance networking at a Blackstar day and have all the Blackstar babes behaving like "Legs n Co"

84. You can't play golf on a links course, fly 500 miles and then be in a meeting in London for 10.00 am.

85. You can't charge **£12,000 a day** for your time - guess you haven't met my good friend **Marcus Cauchi,** for he does!

86. You can't proactively reach out to people you don't know on Ecademy for they'll consider it spam (how ironic is that on a networking site?)

87. You can't use your club home page to beat competitors for a page 1 listing on google

88. You can't use twitter to promote your Ecademy events and test copy on your marketplace ads

89. You can't get 40 marketplace advert headlines written for you (in less than 1hr) specifically to test your new product/service

90. You can't go to a **121 at the Institute of Accountants** and spend 2 hours **telling jokes & doing magic tricks**

91. You can't get an invite to have lunch with a record producer to further your daughter's singing career

92. You can't use Ecademy to get your daughter #1 on google for after a simple keyword term.

93. You can't **produce a video and generate 000s of views on YouTube without paying a London agency to do it.**

94. You can't keep promoting the virtues of academy as part of your core business model, but hey, I'm like that

95. You can't **use academy to beat 10m others for the #1 slot on google** for "business networking club"

96. You can't be a Blackstar on Ecademy for 3 years and not yet had a 121 with Penny Power (ooh a date with penny x)

97. You can't randomly phone Ecademists in other countries and try to help them get PR in their local newspaper

98. You don't think people would drive to 60 miles north of Aberdeen just to pay you to come on your coaching program - the same day they agree to do it (400 mile round trip.) Trust me, it happened ☺;)

99. You can't possibly help an Ecademist win their kids back in a

custody battle, be a witness, give a live testimony and sway the court hearing on the other side of the planet without you physically being in the witness box - Yup it happened

100. You can't match the legendary hospitality of <u>Rory Murray</u>, now **I agree - that is impossible.**

The one thing I really learned from my time on Ecademy though is...

"Be yourself", follow your heart and you never know what you might just achieve especially if you test, test, test all aspects of your social networking and marketing online.

Aye, there's a lot you can achieve with Social Networking, and I've since written a book about my adventures on LinkedIn, a Facebook planner and a social media daily planner. I also plan to share what I've learned in launching a club and group on Facebook.

Can I really write a book about Facebook in 30 days and include the posts, photographs of spotlighted members, the free offers, the results, the introductions, the videos, the stats and graphs and the step by step approach how I did it by May 1st, 2019 - Probably NOT, but hmmmmm, THAT is a challenge, and I think that with your help - anything is possible ☺ ;)

https://www.Facebook.com/groups/growyourbusinessclub/permalink/799187127117251/

 Make a list of the social networks, private membership sites, forums and groups you're currently a member of. Make a list of what you've achieved in them in the last 12 months.

Ode to Social Networkers

An ode to Social Networkers on whichever platform you choose to lurk...

Thank you to my family, I see you each day
Don't say a word, you already have
In your own special way

Thank you to my peers, to each and every one of you
Thank you for your input and seeing it from a different point of view
Thank you for the gift to question, to reflect and to ponder
Its only when we take time out
We really appreciate the wonder
Thank you for the daily lessons, the challenges and the fun
Thank you each and every single one of you
for my work is far from done.

Challenges and Obstacles, they help us in our plight
for opportunities are hidden everywhere,
often visible with hindsight.

Critics come, and critics go
But we should stop and ask, why they think it so
in to our daily lives they do appear
we should spend more time listening but many choose not to hear
We are all a fish in a pond of size
Sometimes it grows before our eyes
But we can grow ourselves from the lessons learned
Why do some still choose to swim against the current?
But first catch your breath, to get in your flow
One deep breath and let it go
Energy doesn't start nor stop that is the norm
It merely changes in its form

Stop counting and measuring, comparing the contrast
Let your hair down, and have a blast
Be true to yourself and have the right attitude
For its starts with yourself and paying gratitude.

Forgive and forget, and wipe the slate clean
Unburden your heart, you know what I mean
be thankful and grateful for all the lessons you've learned
be supportive and helpful to all those concerned.

Stop and reflect on how you have grown
And be thankful for the errors that many have shown.
The next chapter in your life is about to arrive
it's time to embrace it with passion and drive
Thank and forgive and acknowledge the few
that have helped you in your growth and to become the new you.
Thank you.

You just don't know how big this could get...
Join The Evolution, Be The Change You Want to Experience Online.
(I'm in. Are you?)

https://www.Facebook.com/groups/growyourbusinessclub/permalink/
799515070417790/

Join the Evolution

Many business owners use social networking on LinkedIn and Facebook to get leads, get appointments and get sales. Their approach to social networking can be selfish instead of selfless.

If you want to start generating results online. Change your approach.

Stop trying to get, and start giving.

Start sharing that cumulative wisdom you've acquired over the years to demonstrate your knowledge, skills, wisdom you have amassed. In my book "**considering self-employment**" I introduce you to a very powerful exercise to calculate the value of that knowledge and wisdom.

Online, you want to demonstrate the value you offer via your blogs, articles, videos, podcasts, webinars, live streaming events, documents, and of course in your posts in the groups on Facebook.

Be the change you want to experience online.
Join The Evolution that is Grow Your Business Club.

Your Networking Funnel

How you go about your business online is down to you, and many will tell you to sell through the room, NOT to the room, and that includes the virtual room in your browser as you stare at your screen, whichever group, tribe, community or forum you may be in.

However, if you're using Facebook because you are in the B2B arena, then you might just like the following.

Suspects are at the start of your networking funnel, these are the people that appear to be open to being approached, and have a profile or page with their full contact details added. These are the people that you want to target and meet the criteria of the prospect profile that should have created before you start – so you know specifically, who you're targeting. They don't know you exist yet, and there has been no prior contact with them or from them.

Friends (and connections) are suspects who responded to your sales prospecting or social networking activities on Facebook, Twitter or LinkedIn and want to get to know you better. They're like you, are curious about what you have, do and offer. They want to follow you and wish to be connected to you and receive updates from you.

21

Whilst they may have read your profile, you may not have qualified them nor had a chat about how you can help them.

Prospects are the people who meet the criteria in your prospect profile and can help you reach your commercial goals and objectives. These are the people who have requested your FREE Item of value, lead magnet or digital asset (more on that later), and agreed to a chat by phone, by skype or in person. They have confirmed that they are interested in what you offer, but haven't parted with any cash yet.

Clients are people who have invested in the products, services or solutions that you offer. They know you, like you and trust you.

Advocates are usually clients (but not always), they can simply be people you've connected with online (or offline). They're openly promoting (advocating) you and your services to others in their Facebook and LinkedIn networks, and you are reciprocating.

They are recommending you to others in their status updates, group chats, newsletters, videos and webinars and when they use Facebook Live.

Network Partners are the people you are having the most frequent contact with, and have a much higher level of mutual trust. I'd call them HCQPIs. (High Calibre Quantum Potential Individuals). Why? Simply because they're action takers.

Building Relationships using your Networking Funnel *TM*

(Questions to use when connecting your fellow members, and I encourage members of Grow Your Business Club to connect, PM or phone each other. To start building relationships. You'd be surprised just how many business owners are connected to each other on Facebook, but simply don't talk, chat or shoot the breeze.)

What's the biggest project you're working on right now?

How can I help you?

Can you tell me a bit more about what you do?

Who do you know who might be able to help me with?

Who do you know who might be interested in?

If you were me, what would you do?

Who on LinkedIn.com, would you recommend I speak to?

Where on LinkedIn.com, would I find?

How would you like to proceed in taking the next step?

How can we make this happen?

How can we turn this into a win/win?

What do you recommend/advise?

Who would you recommend to….?

Who do you know that is an expert in this field?

Who do you know that is well connected?

What have you found to work well for you?

The above questions are simply guidelines to help you probe, enquire, and seek out the best ways to develop better relationships with all the people you have at the different stages of your network funnel. Your goal is to become better acquainted at each stage.

For me, there are 4 very important things to remember when developing your networking funnel:

1. SELFLESSNESS

   Focus your attention on others – not yourself.

   ## Selflessness

   * Lurkers hunt and are often out to see what they can GET
   * Focus on giving & SHARING. BE SELFLESS – Not Selfish
   * Post content & respond to others' to show the value you offer
   * When you share useful content and ideas, people respond
   * Other people are out to see what they can GET. You're not.

2. RESONANCE

   You will get more people in your network and pipeline who think and act like you.

   ## Resonance

   * People like people who are like them.
   * People like people who think and act like them.
   * People like people who are generous
   * People like people who are practical & helpful
   * People like people who are focused on results

3. FAMILIARITY

People respond better to people they are familiar with, so ensure you get seen (and heard)

Familiarity
※ People do business with people they know, like & trust
※ Join social networking groups online that your audience join
※ On your online profile empathise with your target audience
※ Participate in group discussions and answer questions
※ Share your own experience & value you offer in your posts.

4. RECIPROCITY

No doubt about it – givers gain ;)

Reciprocity
※ People like to receive something of VALUE
※ Those who receive also like to give something in return
※ Learn to pay it forward and be amazed at what happens
※ The more you give, the more you will receive
※ Dont forget to ask for a TOOT, BING, POW or POP in your posts

I like to reinforce the above 4 principles in the club (Group) rules and remind all new members to read the rules in the Group Description, then to introduce themselves and where in the world they're from. I use a wee WELCOME sign to politely get them to engage with me and their fellow members. It also serves to share the ethos of the club and how it will work for them.

After all, Givers Gain, Takers Drain and Lurkers Simply Remain the Same.

Part Two – I love it when a Plan Comes Together

"The Hay Team" ;)

https://www.Facebook.com/fraser.hay.792/videos/10157100587643908/

So, you want to start your own Facebook Group. Decide whether it's for friends, prospects or customers. Decide whether it's for personal or commercial reasons. Think of all the different elements you'll need to consider when planning, creating, engaging and promoting your community. It all starts with a goal, because…

A Dream With a Date Becomes a Goal.
A Goal Broken Down Into Steps Becomes a Plan.
A Plan That Is Actioned Becomes a Reality.
To Turn Your Dreams Into a Reality…
…Take the First Steps TODAY….

Let's Get Serious – Your Group Objectives

I was fortunate enough to generate revenue in the first week of starting my group, and was able to raise an invoice for a 4 figure sum, which I shared in the group. Not to boast, just share that the tactical approach was working.

So question is - what do you want to achieve with your Facebook Group? You need to answer some fundamental questions regarding your business objectives. For example:

Turnover

How much turnover from your Facebook group do you want achieve in the next 12 months?

Go on write it down.

It is worth noting that your group might not be about generating revenue and I get that. ;)

Sales

How many sales do you need to achieve your turnover objectives above? Write it down.

Customers

How many customers do you want to achieve from your group in your next 12 months? Go on, write it down.

Leads / Signups

How many leads or members do you need to generate the sales and revenue you want? If you're not sure then you need to write down what you estimate your closing ratio to be, for example 1 in 3, 1 in 5 or 1 n 10. You then need to multiply that number by how many sales you need.

For example, if you need 100 sales to achieve your revenue objectives and your closing ratio is 1:7, then you would need (100 sales x 7 = 700 leads or members.).

Fans, Friends & Followers

How many people do you want to have in your group and wider network(s) in the next 12 months? Write it down.

Signups / Downloads

Write down how many signups and downloads you want to achieve via your website, webinars or workshops in the next 12 months.

Subscribers

Write down how many newsletter or ezine subscribers you want to achieve in your next 12 months.

Set Your Objectives For The Year Ahead.

 Ensure you have written down each of your objectives above (and any other objectives) that you wish to achieve for the year ahead.

Set Your Objectives For The Month Ahead.

 Divide your Annual objectives by 12 to ensure you have written down each of your objectives that you wish to achieve for the month ahead.

Set Your Objectives For The Week Ahead...

 Divide your Monthly objectives by 4 to ensure you have down each of your objectives that you wish to achieve for the week ahead.

Set Your Objectives For The Day Ahead...

 Divide your Weekly objectives by 7 to ensure you have down each of your objectives that you wish to achieve for the day ahead.

Who do you want to reach?

You need to be very clear in terms of who it is you want to target, reach and engage in your new Facebook group. You need to create a prospect (or ideal client) profile. You need to write down all the criteria that you want your prospective members to meet. You need to be clear on exactly who it is you want to engage with. Read the following points, then create your own prospect profile, search using your ciriteria, reach out and start inviting them into your Facebook Group.

An Ideal B2C Client Profile

If you sell to consumers and individuals and are creating a group for them, then use the following to describe what an ideal "business to consumer" (B2C) client would be to you.
The more detail, the better.

Geographic

- Country, Region, County, City
- Population
- Post Code

Demographic
- Gender
- Age
- Occupation
- Marital Status
- Education
- Income
- Family size
- Home Owner

Psychographic

- Social Status/Class
- Need for status
- Role of money (does it buy material things, self-esteem, etc.?)
- Ethics/"moral compass"
- Risk-taker vs. conservative
- Spendthrift vs. hoarder of money

Sources of suspects who match your profile.

- Facebook.com - Search
- Facebook.com – Group Search

 Use the above info to help you write down and describe what an ideal B2C customer or client would be. You can then give this profile to your advocates.

An Ideal B2B Client Profile

If you operate in the "Business to Business" arena, then use the following to describe an ideal B2B client and the criteria you want them to meet. The more detail, the better.

Geographic

- Country, Region, County, City
- Population
- Post Code

Demographic

- Industry Type (SIC)
- Company Turnover
- No. Employees
- Departments
- Head Office
- Branch
- Single Unit
- SoHO
- Year of Incorp.

Behaviour

- What problems, issues or challenges do they have?
- What impact is this having on their business?
- How can you demonstrate the value of your offering?
- How can you pre-qualify them?
- How do you confirm that they need your help?

Sources of suspects/prospects who fit your profile.

- LinkedIn.com – Check out relevant groups
- Facebook – Check out relevant groups

 Use the above info to help you write down and describe what an ideal B2B customer or client would be. You can then give this profile to your members to help pull, refer, invite and recruit new members into your club.

The 4E Content formula

If you want to be successful with your Facebook group, then you need to ensure you are aware of the 4E formula. So what is it, and how can it help you ensure you get a "return" from your Facebook group marketing activities?

The 4E formula is both simple and practical. It's all about your content and whether it's relevant to your intended group members. So let's now focus in on your content and confirm whether it meets the 4E formula criteria. We expand on your content strategy later in the book,

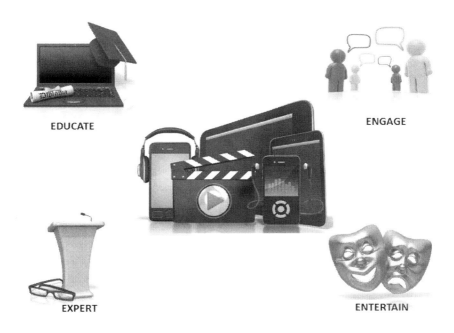

EDUCATE

You want your content in the group to educate your members on how to address and overcome personal, professional or commercial issues, challenges or obstacles. You want to share practical concepts, techniques and ideas that will help them to achieve a specific goal or objective.

 Think about the pains, needs and frustrations your group members may have, and what it is they could benefit from in being educated about. Write it down.

EXPERT

Like above, you want to educate and demonstrate your expertise on a particular topic or subject. You want to share content that you have created and shared in your Facebook Group. This could be presentations, articles, books, courses or videos that you may have created on a relevant topic, issue or subject. (We cover uploading files to your Facebook Group, later.)

 What are you an expert about? What is your area of expertise? What do you want to be known for and what is it that you want to share? Write it down.

ENGAGE

We've touched on this before, but it's important. You want to engage with your members. You need to ask good questions that will encourage your members to respond and engage with you. You may even wish to incentivise or reward your members to answer your questions and share their own views.

Make a list of questions you want to ask your audience. Think about different questions that will encourage your audience to respond and engage with you. Will you want them to use FB Live and engage with you via live video or via the text chat area on the side of your Live Sessions or via Messenger?

ENTERTAIN

Do you want to entertain your audience and members with a live performance? Do you want to share your music? What about your other artistic talents? How can you make your Facebook group an entertaining experience or a memorable one? Think how you can stir the emotions of your audience so they will remember you and your message.

If you want to deliver an entertaining live performance, make a note of what you will include and share to liven up your group, webinar or FB live experience and make it a memorable one.

The Real Cost of Your Facebook Marketing

A few quick questions…

Be honest with me and yourself!

Ready?

Here we go…

 1. How many hours do you spend each week online?
Go on think about it and write it down.

Seriously, how many hours do you spend on your laptop, pc or mobile device?

Write it down.

Done that?

OK Good.

 2. Now write down how much you charge for an hour of your time?
(Either calculate what you charge or what you currently get paid).

Go on write it down.

Done that?

Excellent.

3. Now multiply your answers from questions 1 and 2 to give you a new answer. (Either calculate what you charge or what you currently get paid).

Let's call this No 3. Go on write it down.

That figure is how much of your time you're investing in the management of your online and social media marketing – every week. A bit shocked?

(You should be.)

4. Now multiply the figure you achieved in 3 above by 4 to give you a monthly fee. Write it down.

Finally…

5. Multiply your answer in 4 above (The monthly investment of your time) by **12** to give you an annual figure of what you're investing social media marketing.

Go on write down the figure that you calculated in 5 above.

WOA! Say that number out loud right now.

Say it again out loud – slowly.

Yup, that's how much of your time you'd be investing in online marketing unless you read this book all the way through, and apply the knowledge, suggestions, activities and exercises contained in the pages ahead.

You need to change the way you're managing your social media marketing, especially on Facebook and in your Facebook groups.

You need to come up with a new plan.

You need to make small changes and implement little steps – every single day.

…and if you do, you'll start experiencing real results in no time at all.

Now you know how much your sales prospecting online is costing you in real terms.

Let's look at what you need to do about it, and how you can change the way you manage your prospecting online to start generating real permanent, breakthrough results.

Part Three – Create Your Group

In this section of the book, I want to introduce you to an 11 step plan with some important points to think about to help you get some structure, save time and money in being able to do it all yourself with having to hire a VA, Social Media Techy or someone off of peopleperhour.com

Group Header Graphic

As of the time of writing Graphic Dimensions are 1640 x 856

Struggling to Start or Grow Your Business?
Sign Up to Our FREE Facebook Group Today

GROW YOUR BUSINESS CLUB

What's The Next Goal or Objective That You Want to Achieve? Take Action

- FREE Help, Guidance & Support
- FREE Diagnostic Tools
- FREE Referrals & Introductions
- FREE Webinars & LIVE Meetings
- FREE Member Gifts & Bonuses
- UPGRADE to ∎ BOARDROOM

INVEST IN YOURSELF – JOIN TODAY

www.facebook.com/groups/growyourbusinessclub

Let's do a forensic Analysis of my Header –

1. Qualify Your Group Visitor

2. Add Your Branding Colours & Logo

3. Address the WIFM factor – Tell Them What They're Going to Get

4. The CTA (Call to Action)

As daft as it sounds, many thousands of groups simply don't have a call to action in their graphic header, asking the visitor to join or sign up.

Many just assume that because there is a Join BUTTON on the page, that's it.

Simply remind them what to do.

For people are silently begging to be led. Remember online, the majority of people are Followers.

Creating Your Group – STEP 1

What will the purpose of your group be? What will it be? Who are you targeting and wanting to help? Will be it to a commercial group, a public group, a private group? What will you call it?

When you name your group, think of keywords to add that can help people find your group in the search facility at the top of the page.

Creating Your Group – STEP 2

What will the purpose of your group be? What will it be? Who are you targeting and wanting to help? Will be it to a commercial group, a public group, a private group? What will you call it?

Think how you can add value and help your members, for example I offer members of my group, a FREE Instant Breakthrough using https://bit.ly to shorten the page url to https://www.gybtv.net

Creating Your Group – STEP 3

What Discussions will YOU start? What content will you post?
Visual, Auditory or Kinesthetic?

Will it be text, pictures, photos, videos, slides? Ask questions to
engage your group members.

Think of the different types of posts that you can and will create.
You may want to plan your content, and think about your content
schedule and how often you want to post per day or week.

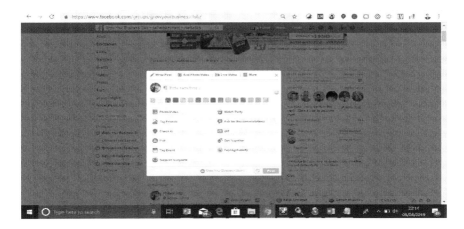

45

Creating Your Group – STEP 4

Have you thought about creating a group chat with you group members? It will enable members.
To get answers in real time, and enable you to go the extra mile with added support for members.

Perhaps you link to your group via your own website or domain. For example, I set up the domain www.growyourbusiness.club, linked it to my group from it, and to a site offering more resources.

Creating Your Group – STEP 5

Have you thought about creating a group chat with you group members? It will enable members
To get answers in real time, and enable you to go the extra mile with added support for members.

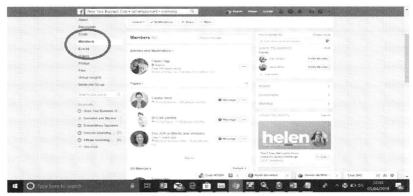

Here you can do something very simple and powerful – that most group owners simply don't do. You can Message individual members and say thank you for joining your group. On the right side of the page, Facebook also recommends people from your network for you to invite to join your group. This can be an excellent quick way for you to build your membership.

Creating Your Group – STEP 6

You can create, post and promote upcoming events for your group and club, and this can be very useful for promoting LIVE events, webinars, courses, workshops or offline member meetings.

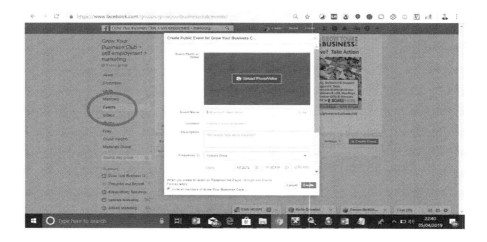

Think about whether you will promote your own events, member events, or simply post a calendar of what's coming up for the month ahead – online and offline to help get registrations & signups.

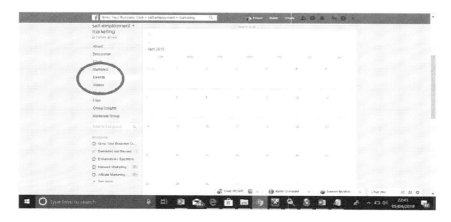

Creating Your Group – STEP 7

You can upload videos to your group to maximize engagement, and to help empathise, educate, wow, woo or impress your audience with testimonials, case studies, and in sharing key principles.

Think how you can encourage, persuade or even incentivise your members to participate and upload their own videos about you, your products, services or solutions or group contribution.

Creating Your Group – STEP 8

Like videos, you can upload photos to your group to maximize engagement, and to help show you, you're products, your services or solutions in action. Encourage your members to do the same.

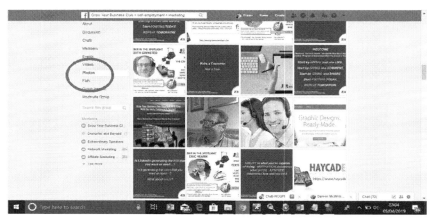

Remember, when it comes to visual graphics, it could be a photograph of a book you've written, or a photo of a book written by a member. It could an infographic or a motivational quote. Think.

Think how you can share, syndicate or promote your images, photos, graphics or infographics on the wider internet and other platforms such as Instagram, Pinterest, slideshare or photobucket.

Creating Your Group – STEP 9

Like videos, and photos, you can also upload files to your group. These files could be PDF or excel files. They might be simple marketing flyers or brochures or detailed course overviews.

Perhaps you have workbooks, student guides for the content in your group or perhaps you have other groups or websites where you offer other coaching, training or consultancy solutions.

51

Creating Your Group – STEP 10

Group Insights can give you invaluable information showing you how well you're doing. The following shows the number of members and amount of engagement in my first 3 weeks of launch.

During this soft launch period and before I started opening my marketing tool box or emptying the "toy cupboard" of all my advanced tools, knowledge and solutions, I learned lots in feedback from members who told me in their posts, emails, PMs and phone calls – reduce the length of my posts.

Creating Your Group – STEP 11

Moderate Group gives you the options to manage, control and protect various aspects of your group, your content, your members and your interactions. Explore it regularly inside your group.

As your group grows think about your post titles, so they become easy to find. Think about your brand, the purpose of your posts and their findability. That's where the SEARCH facility helps.

Part Four – Communicating With Members

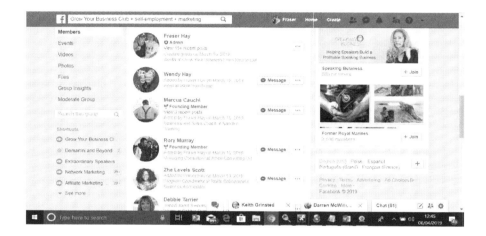

Members are the life blood of your group – You're Raison d'etre. Help them, support them, comment, like and share their posts and guess what – slowly, but surely they begin to roll up their sleeves and take action. It's a team effort after all, and Together Everyone Achieves More.

Are You Losing 66% of Your Members?

When I started my group on Facebook, filled with enthusiasm and a new lease of life after 9 months with my head in a dark place – quite literally, my early posts were loooooonng text based posts.

Your community will soon tell you what they think about your content – either by not engaging or will simply lurk in the background, watching, rolling their eyes and simply not participate.

Let me tell you what I've learned.

People communicate one of three ways –

1. Visually
2. Auditory
3. Kinesthetically

Visually

Many people like to read. They like to absorb what they read. Let it all soak in, before they decide to take action. In my group – Action gets rewarded. Other people prefer to download, print off and then read. What content do you share with your members? Have you thought about uploading PDF, DOCX or XLS files into your group for your members to download or print? But if there's one thing I've learned – Keep your posts short ;)

33% of your members' preferred communication style is **VISUAL.**

Remember this in order to maximize engagement with that segment of your membership. Think what content you can share with your audience. Here are some examples of different types of content for you to think about.

PDF:
https://www.Facebook.com/download/preview/2233207860076274

VIDEO: Encourage, even incentivize your members to UPLOAD video to your group.

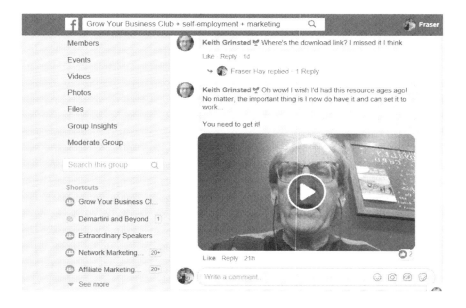

VIDEO: Maybe do a piece to camera and share a personal story & lesson learned.

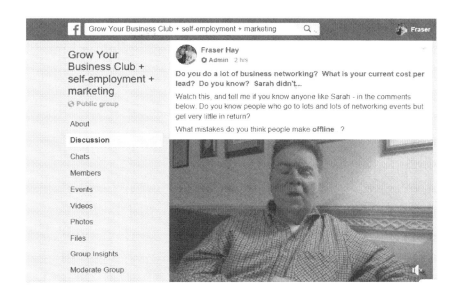

VIDEO: Try creating your own animated videos like this one…

VIDEO: Or this -
https://www.Facebook.com/fraser.hay.792/videos/101570634711489
08/

IMAGE(s): Some example of different images I use in my group:

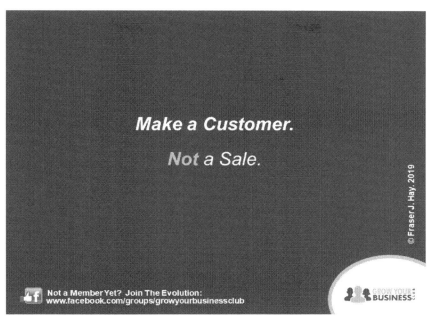

Make a Customer.

Not a Sale.

© Fraser J. Hay, 2019

GROW YOUR BUSINESS CLUB

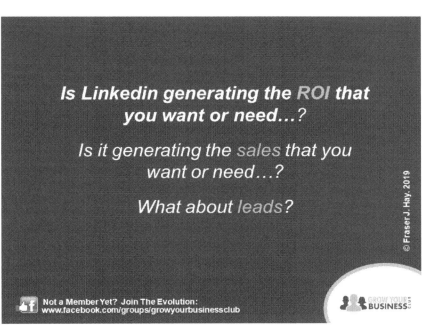

Is Linkedin generating the ROI that you want or need...?

Is it generating the sales that you want or need...?

What about leads?

© Fraser J. Hay, 2019

GROW YOUR BUSINESS CLUB

If you think hiring a
professional is expensive,
wait till you hire an amateur.

© Fraser J. Hay, 2019

GROW YOUR
BUSINESS CLUB

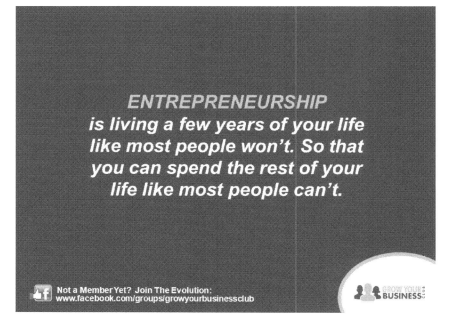

ENTREPRENEURSHIP
is living a few years of your life
like most people won't. So that
you can spend the rest of your
life like most people can't.

GROW YOUR
BUSINESS CLUB

Auditory: some people post podcasts, but with video you get audio & visual…

I even share a FULL webinar about LinkedIn & case studies in the club…

to the full System is here - https://www.gybtv.net/grow-your-business-coaching-sales-pi…/

It's HERE:
https://www.Facebook.com/groups/growyourbusinessclub/permalink/793060774396553/

Kinesthetic – People Buy people, so don't hide behind your browser, tablet or PC, pick up the phone and speak to people or use FB messenger or skype and have real live conversation.

Having a skype call with a member, led to me being one of the speakers alongside some other world class leaders and experts in the virtual Global Referral Summit on 9 - 11 April, 2019

Organised by Outlier Marketing by Pravin Shekar
Others include: Ivan Misner Andy Lopata Bob Burg Matt Ward Chris KentMahua Gorthi Stacey Brown Randall Phil Bedford Mark Layder Michael Griffiths Neeraj Shah Lindsay Adams Susan RoAne Kiruba ShankarSteveBeecham.com and many more...

"My topic - How I generated over 400 testimonials on one social network"
It's going to be a blast ☺ :)

Spread the word & Sign up now: https://tinyurl.com/Referral19

It's amazing how you can create the opportunities you want, when you start engaging with your members, and having conversations to discuss how you can help each other.

Skype, Messenger and FB Live all help you to connect with people in real time, and to develop your relationships as you can, see, hear and feel how you get on and click with each other.

19 Practical Ways to Create Engagement, Members and Sales on Facebook

If you're struggling to generate fans, friends and followers on Facebook, more members for your group or want more likes, engagement and shares, then consider implementing one of these practical tactics each day for the next month. If you find any of them useful, innovative or something you think other people would like, then repeat the tactics daily.

1. Did you just create a new group? Ask everyone and anyone you know to like your group, and sign up and join it. Your objective here is simply to get the ball rolling.

2. Use videos that are only revealed when they like your page. Make sure the videos are very good to excellent - you don't want to disappoint. Short and great is much better than long and boring.

3. Offer a free ebook, but only when they like your page. This is just like offering an ebook for an email address, only with viral possibilities.

4. Run a competition. Run LOTS of competitions. People love contests – they're fun, they get to win stuff, and you don't look like you're promoting but you do build your list – it's a win-win for everyone.

5. Ask questions in your group. Nothing promotes engagement more than asking and responding to people's ideas and especially opinions on a hot topic. In fact, questions get double the rate of comments that statements get.

6. Do you know what's even more powerful than questions? Fill in the blank posts generate 9 times as many comments as regular posts apparently. For example, "The thing I love about social networking is ____"

7. Add a Facebook Social Plugin to your website and blog. Yes, some marketers still haven't done this, yet doing so can result in more exposure, more fans, more business... etc.

8. Ask for a POW, TOOT, BOOM or PING in your group posts ;)

9. Use photos and videos whenever possible. They get shared 2-3 times more than written content. I write about how to create your own videos elsewhere in this book ;)

10. Find places to add a link to your Facebook group. Email signatures are a great one, so are articles, blogposts, other social media, forum signatures, etc.

11. Go for quality over quantity. Start with a small membership and get the engagement happening. Likes are for vanity – Engagement for sanity. 'Nuff said ;)

12. Post news. Anything that is relevant and current for your particular niche. If you look like you are on the breaking edge of what's happening, people will naturally pay attention to all of your Facebook postings. Use Google Alerts to stay abreast of breaking news.

13. The fastest way to grow your group? Tag and involve people. Thank them, introduce them to each other.

14. Rotate your content types and format often. People have different communication and information needs. You've got to keep it interesting, and engaging.

15. Give people a reason to participate in your group. Incentives work great. But even using the word "because" can increase your likes. "Please like our page because we want to impact as many people as possible."

16. Offer something special just to your Facebook group members. For example, a product discount or a special bonus when they purchase your product or service. In Grow Your Business Club, Action Takers Get Rewarded ;)

17. Member promotions? If you're offering a sale, use either the keyword "$ off" or "coupon," since these two keywords tend to produce the highest response. Offering a certain dollar amount off will tend to produce twice the results of offering a certain percentage off of the regular price. Why? Probably because most people don't like math.

18. The shorter the post, the higher the level of engagement. Memorise that rule. That was a lesson I **had** to learn.

19. Post when people aren't working or aren't as busy. User engagement tends to be 20% higher when you post from 8pm to 8am and think of local time zones too.

20. Share other people's stuff. Promote your members. I introduce you to some Grow Your Business Club members elsewhere in the

book. Did you know that when you share someone's content on Facebook, you can create a notification to tell them you shared it?

21. Have an awesome header image. Pay to have this created on peopleperhour.com if you don't have the skills because it makes an excellent first impression.

 Complete the list – by applying one tactic daily for the next 3 weeks or if you're an HCQPI, let's get the show on the road and take ACTION now.

47 Reasons to Use Facebook Live

If you are wondering what you can use Facebook Live for in your Facebook Group and whether it can help you to grow your business online, whilst increasing engagement with your group members, then consider the following points.

With Facebook Live, you can:

1.   Educate clients, members and prospects directly and in real-time
2.   Debate and discuss a current news topic
3.   Get an edge over your competitors and stay ahead of trends, needs and technology
4.   Stay current with members sharing relevant and up-to-date information
5.   Engage members online that are unable to attend your event
6.   Network with like-minded individuals in real time
7.   Increase attendance of your next physical events
8.   Run your own marketing webinars or webcasts
9.   Educate staff in multiple locations all at the same time.
10.   Engage people in real time who are living in remote locations
11.   Interview experts and upload the video to your site or YouTube
12.   Reactivate dormant customers by offering them a FREE GIFT
13.   Interview candidates for jobs
14.   Conduct polls and surveys and get feedback immediately
15.   Reduce your training, learning and development budget
16.   Save money and eliminate travel costs & overnight stays.
17.   Stream your community or charity event out via Facebook live
18.   Add value by making your FB live to members only

19. Improve cash flow by charging for a live streaming event
20. Run a help desk in real-time sorting and addressing client's problems
21. Conduct market research and find out what members want
22. Run your own mastermind in a closed session
23. Conduct a product launch via your own streaming event
24. Run your own "surgery" offering people to take part in a LIVE Q&A
25. Motivate your sales team
26. Share your own negative experience or review of a product.
27. Thank your best members with sharing valuable information
28. Promote your business or network marketing opportunity
29. Keep audience participants engaged for longer.
30. Share a topic that you are passionate about or that is close to your heart.
31. Ask and answer the questions that are important to you
32. Give or receive video testimonials for you, your product & service.
33. Offer a live extract, excerpt or sample of an upcoming workshop.
34. Start and stream your own live event from anywhere.
35. Price test new products and solutions and get live feedback from your audience.
36. Debunk a myth about your product, business, industry or sector.
37. Share case studies and testimonials with your live audience.
38. Inspire and empower others to take responsibility and achieve their (or your) goals.
39. Explain how a particular process works & break it down into simple steps
40. Do a demonstration or "walkthrough" of your product, service or solution.
41. Have someone interview you?
42. Give a motivational or inspiration "piece to camera"

43.   Share a humorous story to help illustrate how you or your solutions can help.

44.   Promote your business opportunity

45.   Build your list by using belive.tv and capture the email address of your attendees

46.   Create your own daily or weekly show on a particular topic.

47.   You can share your videos with others in The Grow Your Business Club Group

Creating Engagement & Increasing Promotion

I created a very simple, practical and powerful system for engaging KEY members and encouraging them to take part in the community. I gave them each a SPOTLIGHT. Please feel free to connect with them via the club and PM them.

I invite you to join Grow Your Business Club, PM each of them and consider how you may be able to work together. Consider inviting them on to your next webinar or speaking at your next event. In my group, action takers get rewarded. As for the lurkers? Well, it's their choice.

Ready? Here you go –

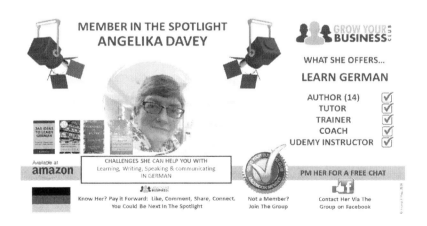

MEMBER IN THE SPOTLIGHT
ANNE QUINN

WHAT DOES ANNE OFFER?

PAIN RELIEF

BACK	☑
LEGS	☑
KNEES	☑
HANDS	☑
FEET	☑

IN PAIN?
ASK ANNE FOR
HELP TODAY

CHALLENGES SHE CAN HELP YOU WITH
Who do you know wants relief from chronic pain?
Contact Anne to find out how she can help you.

PM HER FOR A FREE CHAT

Know Her? Pay it Forward: Like, Comment, Share, Connect.
You Could Be Next In The Spotlight

Not a Member?
Join The Group

Contact HER Via The
Group on Facebook

MEMBER IN THE SPOTLIGHT
DARREN McWILLIAM

WHAT HE OFFERS...

TECH WIZARD

WEBSITE DESIGN	☑
APP DESIGN	☑
SOFTWARE	☑
CONSULTANCY	☑
TRAVEL VLOGGING	☑

Has Rucksack,
Laptop, Gorgeous
Girlfriend & Passport.
Read His Incredible
True Story Inside
The Club

https://www.faramagan.com/

SELF-EMPLOYMENT?

CHALLENGES HE CAN HELP YOU WITH
If you need a technical solution to help you automate
Your small business and grow online – PM HIM

PM HIM FOR A FREE CHAT

Know Him? Pay it Forward: Like, Comment, Share, Connect.
You Could Be Next In The Spotlight

Not a Member?
Join The Group

Contact Him Via The
Group on Facebook

MEMBER IN THE SPOTLIGHT
DEBORAH MEREDITH

WHAT SHE OFFERS...

EMPOWERING WOMEN

AUTHOR	☑
KEYNOTE SPEAKER	☑
COACH	☑
ACTRESS & PRESENTER	☑
CHANGER OF LIVES	☑

Her Mantra
"Whatever it Takes"

Whatever It Takes

https://notarehearsal.co.uk/

Available at
amazon

CHALLENGES SHE CAN HELP YOU WITH
At a Crossroads? In an unhappy relationship?
Uncertain about your future? Lack Confidence?

PM HER FOR A FREE CHAT

Know Her? Pay it Forward: Like, Comment, Share, Connect.
You Could Be Next In The Spotlight

Not a Member?
Join The Group

Contact Her Via The
Group on Facebook

MEMBER IN THE SPOTLIGHT
Dr. JOY MADDEN

GROW YOUR
BUSINESS CLUB

WHAT SHE OFFERS...

HOME ENHANCEMENT

AUTHOR & EDITOR	☑
WINDOWS & DOORS	☑
BLINDS & SHUTTERS	☑
LIVING SPACE	☑
AWNINGS	☑
CARROM CHAMPION	☑

Available at
amazon

CHALLENGES SHE CAN HELP YOU WITH
If you require to modernise, brighten, secure, protect
or add value to your property then get in touch

PM HER FOR A CHAT TODAY

Know Her? Pay It Forward: Like, Comment, Share, Connect.
You Could Be Next In The Spotlight

Not a Member?
Join The Group

HER WEBSITE
https://joyofblindsandshutters.co.uk/

MEMBER IN THE SPOTLIGHT
DR. SIMON RAYBOULD

GROW YOUR
BUSINESS CLUB

WHAT HE OFFERS...

PRESENTATION SKILLS

BEST SELLING AUTHOR	☑
KEYNOTE SPEAKER	☑
TRAINING	☑
COACHING	☑
CONSULTANCY	☑

Available at
amazon

CHALLENGES HE CAN HELP YOU WITH
Public Speaking, Presenting, Communicating.
WOW, EDUCATE & WOO YOUR AUDIENCE

PM HIM FOR A FREE CHAT

Know Him? Pay It Forward: Like, Comment, Share, Connect.
You Could Be Next In The Spotlight

Not a Member?
Join The Group

Contact Him Via The
Group on Facebook

MEMBER IN THE SPOTLIGHT
ERIC HEARN

GROW YOUR
BUSINESS CLUB

WHAT HE OFFERS...

TEXTILE PRINTING

LANYARDS	☑
BELTS & LACES	☑
SPORTS TRIMS	☑
WEBBINGS	☑
BARRIERS	☑

Owner of the
UK's Largest
Narrow Fabric
Printing Business

http://atlastransfer.co.uk

CHALLENGES HE CAN HELP YOU WITH
If you're planning a corporate event, sports event or
festival & need lanyards, contact Eric

PM HIM FOR A FREE CHAT

Know Him? Pay It Forward: Like, Comment, Share, Connect.
You Could Be Next In The Spotlight

Not a Member?
Join The Group

Contact Him Via The
Group on Facebook

CLUB FOUNDER
Fraser J. Hay

H C Q P I

WHAT DOES HE OFFER...?

VENTURE CATALYST

AUTHOR (18)	☑
LIFE COACH	☑
BUSINESS COACH	☑
MARKETING COACH	☑
KEYNOTE SPEAKER	☑
CONSULTANT	☑

Available at
amazon

CHALLENGES HE CAN HELP YOU WITH
Identify what's holding you back & preventing you
from achieving your entrepreneurial goals & objectives

PM HIM VIA THE CLUB

Pay it Forward: Like, Comment, Share, Connect.
You Could Be Next In The Spotlight

Not a Member?
Join The Group

HIS WEBSITE
www.growyourbusiness.club

MEMBER IN THE SPOTLIGHT
HARUN RABBANI

WHAT HE OFFERS...

MOTIVATIONAL
SPEAKER

MIND	☑
BODY	☑
SOUL	☑
LIFESTYLE	☑
SUCCESS	☑

Available at
amazon

CHALLENGES HE CAN HELP YOU WITH
Want to transform your mind, body & soul, Listen
to his podcasts, read his book & attend his Keynotes

PM HIM FOR A FREE CHAT

Know Him? Pay it Forward: Like, Comment, Share, Connect.
You Could Be Next In The Spotlight

Not a Member?
Join The Group

Contact Him Via The
Group on Facebook

MEMBER IN THE SPOTLIGHT
KEITH GRINSTED

WHO'S KEITH?...

THE OLDERPRENEUR

AUTHOR	☑
GHOST WRITER	☑
LINKEDIN DYNAMO	☑
SOCIAL MEDIA BOD	☑
OVER 50's SUPPORTER	☑

ASK KEITH FOR
HELP TODAY

https://www.olderpreneur.co.uk/the-olderpreneur-club

CHALLENGES HE CAN HELP YOU WITH
Over 50? Semi-Retired? Catching Your Breath & Ready
To venture online even start your own business?

PM HIM FOR A FREE CHAT

Know Him? Pay it Forward: Like, Comment, Share, Connect.
You Could Be Next In The Spotlight

Not a Member?
Join The Group

Contact Him Via The
Group on Facebook

MEMBER IN THE SPOTLIGHT
NIGEL RISNER

GROW YOUR BUSINESS CLUB

WHAT HE OFFERS...

MOTIVATIONAL SPEAKER

Business Speaker
Of The Year.
Worked
More than
1,000,000
people

GROUPS 5 TO 5000 ✓
KEYNOTE SPEAKER ✓
AUTHOR ✓
PRESENTER ✓
BROADCASTER ✓

https://www.nigelrisner.com/

CHALLENGES HE CAN HELP YOU WITH
Create an I.M.P.A.C.T. and Develop Your Team to Lead
Your Organisation Through Transformational Change

PM HIM FOR A FREE CHAT

Know Him? Pay it Forward: Like, Comment, Share, Connect.
You Could Be Next In The Spotlight

Not a Member?
Join The Group

Contact Him Via The
Group on Facebook

MEMBER IN THE SPOTLIGHT
PAUL LANGE

GROW YOUR BUSINESS CLUB

WHAT HE OFFERS...

MENTORING

COACHING ✓
MENTORING ✓
MINDFULNESS ✓
PERSONAL ✓
DEVELOPMENT ✓
ENTREPRENEURSHIP ✓

CHALLENGES HE CAN HELP YOU WITH
Starting, Growing or Selling Your Business.
BUSINESS TRANSFORMATION MENTORSHIP

PM HIM FOR A FREE CHAT

Know Him? Pay it Forward: Like, Comment, Share, Connect.
You Could Be Next In The Spotlight

Not a Member?
Join The Group

HIS WEBSITE
https://paullange.com.au

MEMBER IN THE SPOTLIGHT
RED O' LAUGHLIN

GROW YOUR BUSINESS CLUB

WHOS IS HE...

PROSPERITY PROFESSOR

BEST SELLING AUTHOR ✓
PUBLIC SPEAKER ✓
RESEARCHER ✓
HEALTH & WELLNESS ✓
PERSONAL GROWTH ✓

https://www.redolaughlin.com/

Available at
amazon

CHALLENGES HE CAN HELP YOU WITH
Information to treat the causes and not the symptoms
of key health issues and provide you with solutions

PM HIM FOR A FREE CHAT

Know Him? Pay it Forward: Like, Comment, Share, Connect.
You Could Be Next In The Spotlight

Not a Member?
Join The Group

Contact Him Via The
Group on Facebook

MEMBER IN THE SPOTLIGHT
MR. RORY MURRAY

GROW YOUR BUSINESS CLUB

WHAT HE OFFERS...

ENTERPRISE ARCHITECT
(& MORE)

AUTHOR	☑
IT SPECIALIST	☑
TOGAF ARCHITECT	☑
PROCESS ANALYST	☑
WORLD CLASS	☑

Available at
amazon

CHALLENGES HE CAN HELP YOU WITH
Transformational Project leadership, Business Planning,
Strategic Development, Risk Management & MORE

PM HIM FOR A FREE CHAT

Know Him? Pay it Forward: Like, Comment, Share, Connect.
You Could Be Next In The Spotlight

Not a Member?
Join The Group

Contact Him Via The
Group on Facebook

MEMBER IN THE SPOTLIGHT
SHAMUS DOHERTY

GROW YOUR BUSINESS CLUB

WHAT HE OFFERS...

PERSONAL TRAINER

FITNESS COACH	☑
LIFESTYLE COACH	☑
WEIGHT LOSS	☑
NUTRITION ADVICE	☑
FACE TO FACE	☑
& ONLINE	☑

Shay Fit
Get Fit, Stay Fit, Shay Fit

CHALLENGES HE CAN HELP YOU WITH
Sustainable Weight Loss Without Having to Visit a Gym.

PM HIM FOR A CHAT TODAY

Know Him? Pay it Forward: Like, Comment, Share, Connect.
You Could Be Next In The Spotlight

Not a Member?
Join The Group

HIS WEBSITE
https://shayfit.co.uk/

MEMBER IN THE SPOTLIGHT
STEVE PONTON

GROW YOUR BUSINESS CLUB

WHAT HE OFFERS...

ADVICE & SUPPORT

TAX INVESTIGATIONS	☑
EMPLOYMENT	☑
CRISIS MANAGEMENT	☑
ONLINE PAYMENTS	☑
DEBT MANAGEMENT	☑
HEALTH & SAFETY	☑

Run a Small
Business in
or around
EDINBURGH?

CHALLENGES HE CAN HELP YOU WITH
If you require advice, support or even finance to help
you run, manage & grow your business

PM HIM TO SAVE MONEY TODAY

Know Him? Pay it Forward: Like, Comment, Share, Connect.
You Could Be Next In The Spotlight

Not a Member?
Join The Group

HIS WEBSITE
www.fsb.org.uk

MEMBER IN THE SPOTLIGHT
STEVEN GARDINER

GROW YOUR **BUSINESS** CLUB

WHAT HE OFFERS...

AERIAL MEDIA

AERIAL VIDEO	☑
AERIAL PHOTOGRAPHY	☑
STRUCTURAL SURVEYS	☑
CHIMNEYS. MASTS. SPIRES	☑
CAA APPROVED	☑

Do You Need a Stunning Video, Photograph, Detailed Analysis or a Corporate Promotional Video from Above?

https://www.rotorworx.co.uk

CHALLENGES HE CAN HELP YOU WITH
If you need a professional, licensed CAA Approved DRONE operator to film from an elevated position

PM HIM FOR A FREE CHAT

Know Him? Pay it Forward: Like, Comment, Share, Connect.
You Could Be Next In The Spotlight

Not a Member?
Join The Group

Contact Him Via The
Group on Facebook

MEMBER IN THE SPOTLIGHT
STEVEN HEALEY

GROW YOUR **BUSINESS** CLUB

WHAT HE OFFERS...

WEB BROADCASTING

AUTHOR	☑
LIVE STREAMING	☑
TECHNICAL ADVICE	☑
TRAINING	☑
CONSULTANCY	☑

Available at
amazon

CHALLENGES HE CAN HELP YOU WITH
Planning, Presenting & Promoting Your
LIVE STREAMING EVENTS

PM HIM FOR A FREE CHAT

Know Him? Pay it Forward: Like, Comment, Share, Connect.
You Could Be Next In The Spotlight

Not a Member?
Join The Group

Contact Him Via The
Group on Facebook

MEMBER IN THE SPOTLIGHT
WARREN WILSON

GROW YOUR **BUSINESS** CLUB

WHAT HE OFFERS...

SUCCESSFUL INVENTOR

AUTHOR	☑
PROBLEM SOLVER	☑
CREATIVE DYNAMO	☑
PATENTS	☑
IDEA TO $45m REALITY	☑

FREE ON HIS WEBSITE

https://warrenwilsoninventor.com/

CHALLENGES HE CAN HELP YOU WITH
Got an idea? Want to Protect it & Turn it into a $45m brand reality. Warren Did. Now he can help you.

PM HIM FOR A FREE CHAT

Know Him? Pay it Forward: Like, Comment, Share, Connect.
You Could Be Next In The Spotlight

Not a Member?
Join The Group

Contact Him Via The
Group on Facebook

MEMBER IN THE SPOTLIGHT
ELSABE SMIT

GROW YOUR BUSINESS CLUB

WHAT SHE OFFERS...

RENOWNED PSYCHIC

Why Doubt or Struggle When You Can Have Answers.

AUTHOR (16 Books)	☑
PSYCHIC	☑
COACH	☑
TV PRESENTER	☑
KEYNOTE SPEAKER	☑
ENERGY HEALING	☑

PM HER FOR A FREE READING

CHALLENGES SHE CAN HELP YOU WITH
Business/Personal Decisions. Challenging Relationships
Coping, Planning & Responding to Change.

Pay it Forward: Like, Comment, Share, Connect.
You Could Be Next In The Spotlight

Not a Member?
Join The Group

HER WEBSITE
www.elsabesmit.com

MEMBER IN THE SPOTLIGHT
IAIN WHYTE

GROW YOUR BUSINESS CLUB

THE SOLUTION HE OFFERS

COACHING HELP

Givers Gain
Takers Drain
Lurkers Simply
Remain The Same

AUTHOR	☑
BNI TRAINER	☑
COACH	☑
CONSULTANT	☑
KEYNOTE SPEAKER	☑
FSB MEMBERSHIP	☑

CHALLENGES HE CAN HELP YOU WITH
Facing personal or commercial challenges?
How to transform your lifestyle.

Pay it Forward: Like, Comment, Share, Connect.
You Could Be Next In The Spotlight

Not a Member?
Join The Group

HIS WEBSITE
Bigmantalking.com

MEMBER IN THE SPOTLIGHT
MARCUS CAUCHI

GROW YOUR BUSINESS CLUB

THE SOLUTION HE OFFERS

SALES TRAINING

Givers Gain
Takers Drain
Lurkers Simply
Remain The Same

AUTHOR	☑
TRAINER	☑
COACH	☑
CONSULTANT	☑
KEYNOTE SPEAKER	☑

CHALLENGES HE CAN HELP YOU WITH
Sales Management, Channel Sales,
Recruiting, Motivating or Firing Your Sales Team

Pay it Forward: Like, Comment, Share, Connect.
You Could Be Next In The Spotlight

Not a Member?
Join The Group

HIS WEBSITE
www.southeast.sandler.com

MEMBER IN THE SPOTLIGHT
Zhe L. Scott

GROW YOUR BUSINESS CLUB

HOW CAN SHE HELP YOU?

SEO
CONSULTANT

AUTHOR ☑
SPEAKER ☑
MUSICIAN ☑
FREE CHAT ☑

Givers Gain
Takers Drain
Lurkers Simply
Remain The Same

Pay it Forward: Like, Comment, Share, Connect.
You Could Be Next In The Spotlight

Not a Member?
Join The Group

HER WEBSITE
www.theseoqueen.net

MEMBER IN THE SPOTLIGHT
JIM AITKEN

GROW YOUR BUSINESS CLUB

WHAT HE OFFERS...

ADVICE & SUPPORT

TAX INVESTIGATIONS ☑
EMPLOYMENT ☑
CRISIS MANAGEMENT ☑
ONLINE PAYMENTS ☑
DEBT MANAGEMENT ☑
HEALTH & SAFETY ☑

Run a Small
Business in
The Highlands
of Scotland?

CHALLENGES HE CAN HELP YOU WITH
If you require advice, support or even finance to help
you run, manage & grow your business

PM HIM TO SAVE MONEY TODAY

Know Him? Pay it Forward: Like, Comment, Share, Connect.
You Could Be Next In The Spotlight

Not a Member?
Join The Group

HIS WEBSITE
www.fsb.org.uk

MEMBER IN THE SPOTLIGHT
KAREL FRIELINK

GROW YOUR BUSINESS CLUB

WHAT HE OFFERS...

LEGAL HELP

MANAGING PARTNER ☑
CORPORATE LAW ☑
CORP. GOVERNANCE ☑
FINANCE LAW ☑
BANKING ☑
HOSPITALITY ☑

FraudNet
Legal Network
MEMBER

CHALLENGES HE CAN HELP YOU WITH
If you require a top legal firm in Curacao, to address
COMPLEX INTERNATIONAL FRAUD MATTERS

PM HIM FOR A FREE CHAT

Know Him? Pay it Forward: Like, Comment, Share, Connect.
You Could Be Next In The Spotlight

Not a Member?
Join The Group

CONTACT HIM
VIA LINKEDIN

The secret to making the SPOTLIGHTS effective, was that I tagged them in an introduction post so that they were mentioned in a post in the group that also appeared on their news feed.

I then promoted them on LinkedIn, and tagged them into LinkedIn and used #HASHTAGS.

Did it work – Very quickly the views started to rise individually for them on Facebook & LinkedIn.

This was just one spotlight, on one platform that I used in the soft launch before I wanted to ramp up and roll out a full blown marketing campaign. None of my Grow Your Business School Tools or Grow Your Business Boardroom resources were used – or those I share in my Social Media Daily Planner Course or Pipeline Programme.

Create Even More Engagement

A simple, powerful and proven tactic is to introduce your group members to each other. Very quickly, members start taking the initiative themselves, relationships are formed, conversations and appointments generated, business conducted and money earned.

Something else I do is recommend my members' books. I have an extensive personal library of over 1000 books and love learning from other professionals. I goto Amazon, purchase their book and sometimes take a quick photo of the latest member book I have purchased and read.

Here are a selection of books I recommend -

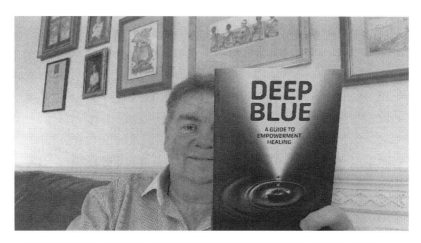

How to Welcome Your NEW Members

A simple, powerful and proven tactic when a NEW member joins, is to write a post asking your fellow members to welcome their new addition, ensuring your TAG the new member so they see the announcement on their feed and your members will get an update about it too.

Something else I recommend to help with engagement is to ask them to post where in the world they're from, and to share 3 fun facts about themselves – All adds to the ethos of the community.

It's also a feature of a group in being to write a post to introduce ALL new members. Cool, eh?

How to Save Time & Money

Something I recommend you do to save time as your group grows, is create a wee ASCII TXT file and store some of your commonly used email messages, messenger chats, and common or frequent posts in your group or on the wider internet.

Here's a wee checklist to help you save time and maximize your results.

1. Invitation email or messenger chat for your connections and friends to join your group

Hi I have set up a new group to help people raise their profile and spread the word about what they offer - including your good self. It's HERE and it would be good to see you inside - https://www.Facebook.com/groups/growyourbusinessclub

2. Welcome Post -

Please Give a Warm Welcome to:

[NAME]

Read the rules in the club description, Click the following link & introduce yourself & where in the world you're from. Give us 3 fun facts about your good self and how you think you can help your fellow members and they - you.

Oh, and the link is HERE - http://xxxxxxxxxxxxxxxxxxxxxxxx

3. Keep a note of the URLs of your favourite posts
4. Keep a note of the URL to testimonials and case studies

5. Personal touch, following up via Messenger reinforcing your ethos & group rules

The secret to winning biz in the club is to SHARE SHARE SHARE and demonstrate just how good u are without PITCHING or spamming - folk will appreciate what you have to offer. The secret is to sell through the club NOT TO THE CLUB, for once they recognise just how good u are - WOA, you'll get great profile and business in due course ;) P.S. Do read the club rules and ethos in the group description ;) And we must catch up for a wee chat on tel or skype at some point ;)

6. Personal touch, following up NEW Members who maybe lurking & not engaging - yet

Hi [NAME], welcome to the club. I hope you're settling in ok. Please feel free to welcome the new members, and share some of your own knowledge, talent and experience in the club. And if you need anything, please - just ask ;)

7. Struggling to find good copyright free photos for your posts? Use www.pixabay.com

8. Struggling to find good copyright free Videos for your posts? Use www.pixabay.com

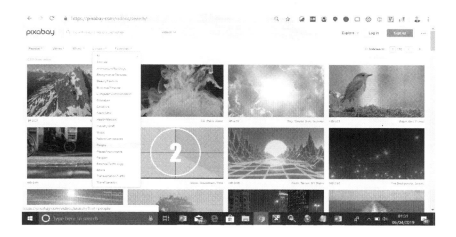

9. Create, design and post eye catching content for FREE with www.canva.com

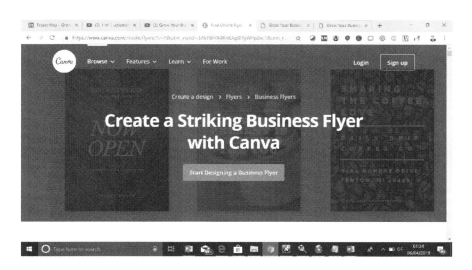

How to Create Stunning Videos Using PowerPoint in 30 minutes or Less

Here's a quick example of a video I created using PowerPoint in under half an hour, exported it, then uploaded to my group...

The video is HERE -
https://www.Facebook.com/fraser.hay.792/videos/10157097963683908/

Many More examples are in the video section of my group -
https://www.Facebook.com/groups/growyourbusinessclub/videos/

Watch this quick short video. It's a wee example of creating a simple video, and then we'll talk about the 4 simple components that pull it all together...

https://youtu.be/IlvVMeBlQUY

That video was created using POWERPOINT, and there only 4 key elements:-

- Images
- Animations
- Transitions
- Music

Remember, the FREE resource I shared earlier in the book -

That LinkedIn Logo rotating above at the start of that video uses the SWIVEL animation. In fact, there are many different animations you can choose, for example -

You can add a background and make it appear to grow using the GROW/SHRINK animation. Watch the woman's eyes in this video...

Once you've created your video in POWERPOINT, you simple EXPORT to mp4. Seemples.

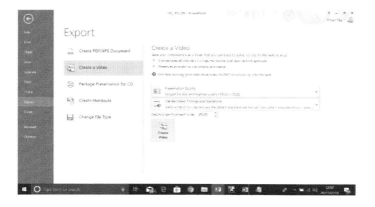

And before you know it, it's coming up page 1 on generic google results - EPIC ;)

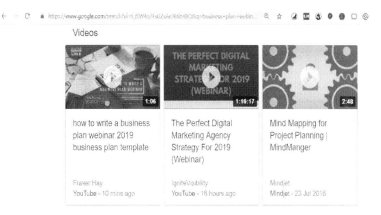

Videos

how to write a business plan webinar 2019 business plan template	The Perfect Digital Marketing Agency Strategy For 2019 (Webinar)	Mind Mapping for Project Planning	MindManger
Fraser Hay YouTube - 10 mins ago	IgniteVisibility YouTube - 16 hours ago	Mindjet Mindjet - 23 Jul 2018

Need help in creating your own videos or marketing message, contact me via the group.

What is the next marketing goal or objective that you want to achieve? Get in touch.

Inspired by my house for sale video, Grow Your Business Club Member, Christine Miller gave me a TOOT via a PM in wanting to find out how she could create her own video? The result?

Watch her wee video here –

https://www.Facebook.com/groups/growyourbusinessclub/permalink/801778576858106/

Part Five – Marketing Outside Your Group

This section of the book will hopefully turn your attention to marketing outside the group. I have many other books on Amazon that cover this in detail, coaching programs and The Lead Generation MBA course. If you want more members, then you need to take action – It's that simple. I share lots of different tools from the tool box and toys from the toy cupboard at www.gybtv.net, but in the meantime…

The single biggest mistake in Facebook Marketing & Running Groups

Yes you need to target, invite and signup new members to your group, but stop practicing "Selfish Prospecting" or "Selfish Marketing".

Quite often, inviting members to their group, for many small business owners just doesn't work, because they are trying to **GET** new customers...

All their energy and time is spent on trying to **GET** NEW customers to work with them.

Ironically, by trying to **GET** new customers, your sales and marketing messages actually end up pushing them away...

Why is this case?

You probably **NEED** new customers and WANT more business. Yes?

Believe it or not, but this is reflected in all your prospecting activities.

- **It's reflected in your status updates, articles and group posts.**
- **It's reflected in your emails.**
- **It's reflected in your skype chats, Personal Messages & LIVE messages!**

Think. How many times have you gone to a networking event and met someone who you thought NEEDED the business?

How many times have you met people at networking events offline that you thought they were desperate for business? At networking events offline, how many times has someone given you a business card before you asked for it, and you never called them back? It's the same online.

What about when you keep reading status updates on Facebook or LinkedIn – "Buy from me. Buy from me."

You know what I mean. It happens all the time.

If you subconsciously are aware of this - **THEN SO ARE YOUR PROSPECTS and MEMBERS of your group.**

Your members have a "Desperation" detector, and what's worse when you are in NEED of new business, you actually end up focusing on YOU - not the member or prospect.

Many Facebook marketers don't realise it, but...

In all their marketing communications, emails, blog posts, article writing, and phone calls to previous clients it's all about THEM and WHAT THEY DO.

Worse still, they end up focusing all their marketing on what they KNOW, what they

HAVE and what they DO.

They go into great detail about their products, services, and what makes them different. Don't you make the same mistake. For, by focusing on yourself, you become oblivious to everyone else and their pains, needs, wants and frustrations. Everyone else isn't interested in what you have, do or know, because they're preoccupied with their own problems, needs and wants.

Many marketers on Facebook are simply pre-occupied with what <u>they</u> have, do or know.

Does any of this sound familiar?

- You're not getting the replies you want to your status updates, or videos.
- You're leaving a lot of messages on voice mail.
- You're not getting the appointments from your follow-ups after those networking meetings or after you've added people to your Facebook connections.

If so, then you're beginning to think that prospecting on Facebook doesn't work.

You're almost right.

Selfish prospecting doesn't work well online.

Ironically, the more selfish prospecting you do, the more cynical and skeptical you become to social networking and social media marketing and end up convincing yourself it is a complete waste of time, and it begins to really affect your attitude not just to marketing but to doing business in general. You might get the odd phone call from an existing client that helps to stop the famine, but this feast and famine scenario is constantly repeating itself in regular sales cycles (or lack of sales) cycles.

…but there's good news.

You could change your approach, and begin to start generating INSTANT results with your Facebook group marketing.

For example

- Remind your prospects of their problems and how you can help
- Ask your prospects questions instead of talking about you
- Offer something for FREE upfront to demonstrate that you excel at what you do

More importantly, you could change your entire focus from GETTING to **GIVING**.

You need to start giving and sharing valuable advice, information and "**FREE ITEMS OF VALUE**" in all your sales and marketing communications online to help your prospects.

That way all your marketing activities are focused on the needs, problems and frustrations of your prospective clients - not **you.** Start offering valuable and useful information and resources to your members   today.

Spend little or no time talking about you or what you **DO** or **HAVE**.

Remind your members of their pain, needs and frustrations, and they will become very interested in what you offer, for you offer a SOLUTION that can solve their problems.

Encourage your members to talk about and share their problems, pains and issues in your group. Let them share their passions as well.

Remember your LinkedIn Profile or website should do all the qualifying. Your sales goal online is simply want members to seek out, visit and read your profile or website page – that's it. More on that later.

At networking events offline, you shouldn't spend 5-10 minutes talking about **you** and what you **do**. You succinctly articulate what it is you offer, and then direct pertinent qualifying, fact finding questions to your prospect, to get them talking about what they KNOW, DO or HAVE.

You DO NOT want to rush to give people your card and have them dreading your follow up phone call the next day you will want to gently probe, enquire, and find out a little more about your prospect by asking good exploratory questions.

..And **if the answers they give you fit your criteria of an ideal member**, then you will ask prospects for their card and tell them you're going to send them something for FREE in the next day or so, that will find of value and interest.

Guess what?

- They will now want to give you their card or personal details.
- They now look forward to your call.
- They will look forward to the FREE item of value you're going to send them.

Ensure you prevent becoming a victim of selfish prospecting for members online or offline.

Start offering FREE items of value like a FREE membership to your Facebook Group.

Start giving more value upfront. **You can also integrate this technique into your online, social and tele-marketing too, if you want to. Invite people to join your group.**

If you're not generating the results you want from your sales prospecting online, then you're going to have to change your "M.O."

– your modus operandi; the way you go about selling what you have to offer your target market. The secret is to be proactively helpful sharing good useful content, suggestions and ideas whilst reciprocating positively wherever and whenever you can.

Remember the mantra I shared earlier? It's so true.

"Givers Gain, Takers Drain and Lurkers Simply Remain The Same."

50+ additional Ways to Promote Your NEW Facebook Group

If you want to raise awareness of your NEW Facebook Group and want to start building your membership then simply select one of the suggestions below and execute it.

Just remember reading an idea or suggestion is one thing, but rolling up your sleeves and executing or implementing it is another. After all, knowledge is not power, but applied knowledge is.

Please go through the list. Many of the ideas can also be used to promote your specific products, services or solutions and not just the group for building your tribe, community or following.

Ready?

Let's begin...

- ✓ Create a new email signature and add details of your NEW Group
- ✓ Add a widget or ad about your group to the home page of your site
- ✓ Write a status update on LinkedIn and share it with your network
- ✓ Write a press release - check out prweb.com
- ✓ Mention it in your newsletter or e-zine
- ✓ Add a popup box or slide-in box on your site to promote the group

- ✓ Create a video trailer for your group and share it on Facebook or LinkedIn
- ✓ Create an infographic and upload it Facebook or LinkedIn
- ✓ Ask your contacts on LinkedIn or Facebook to join or share the registration page url
- ✓ Add your uploaded media from slideshare.net to your LinkedIn Profile
- ✓ Start a Facebook page about the upcoming group offering additional support
- ✓ Do a status update on LinkedIn, twitter & Facebook
- ✓ Join peer groups on LinkedIn and share your status update about the group
- ✓ Upload a video to Vimeo
- ✓ Use pingler.com to promote all your group url
- ✓ Encourage group members to write or give video testimonials
- ✓ Ask for 2 referrals from existing group members
- ✓ Re-write your profile on LinkedIn to promote your group
- ✓ Click on a 100 members' profiles in a LI Group & let LI pull them to your profile.
- ✓ Write a blog about your upcoming group on Facebook
- ✓ Tweet about your group or add a status update on Facebook
- ✓ Create a podcast about your upcoming group with blogtalkradio.com
- ✓ Create a promotional JPG or PNG & share via your existing Facebook groups
- ✓ Add a media gallery to your LI profile and add them to slideshare too
- ✓ Find potential JV partner's via LinkedIn's advanced search to share your group
- ✓ Ask a local office supply company to include your leaflet in their catalogue
- ✓ Offer a loss leader, Free item of value or a digital asset
- ✓ Promote with photos and images on Pinterest
- ✓ Create a survey to find out what people want an group about

- ✓ Create a schedule of groups with an group plugin for your site
- ✓ Visit www.growyourbusiness.club
- ✓ Ask other companies to put your leaflet out with their statements/catalogue
- ✓ Promote your group via reddit
- ✓ Ask your clients to mail their list
- ✓ Ask your suppliers to mail their list promoting your upcoming group
- ✓ Upload a video to Vimeo
- ✓ Sign up to growyourbusiness.club
- ✓ Advertise on Google ad words
- ✓ Ask fellow bloggers to give your group a mention
- ✓ Upload a video to dailymotion.com
- ✓ Update your author page on amazon.com and goodreads.com
- ✓ Create a lens on squidoo.com
- ✓ Share your group local community groups on Facebook
- ✓ Use your affiliate network
- ✓ Promote your group on the footer of your site
- ✓ Share details at https://www.Facebook.com/groups/blabnation/
- ✓ Publicise your group in your local chamber of commerce newsletter
- ✓ Use a group specific hashtag
- ✓ Tweet your group and link to your registration page
- ✓ Ask fellow webcasters to promote your group mailing their list
- ✓ Get interviewed about your upcoming group
- ✓ Create a killer landing page on your site
- ✓ Do a FREE Ad swap with another e-zine or newsletter owner
- ✓ Share details of your next webinar about the group in your favourite forums
- ✓ Consider advertising on LinkedIn or Facebook then Boost Your Ad
- ✓ Add your group as a project on your LinkedIn Profile

- ✓ Run a competition to a membership to your PAID group
- ✓ Create a voice mail message to promote your group
- ✓ Create an out-of-the-office auto email message about your group
- ✓ In your talks & presentations, conclude by telling them about your group
- ✓ Blog asking for guest speakers in your group webinars & events
- ✓ Post inviting members from LinkedIn Groups to join your group on Facebook
- ✓ Post inviting members in other Facebook groups to join your group
- ✓ Ask group members on LinkedIn what topics they'd like a group about
- ✓ Ask group members on Facebook what topics they'd like a group about
- ✓ Use Instagram to promote your group
- ✓ Add details of your group on your company page on LinkedIn
- ✓ Send an SMS message to your phone contacts to invite them to your group
- ✓ Create a custom url for the group or register a new domain and point it to the group
- ✓ Speak at a networking group and tell them about your upcoming group
- ✓ Speak at tradeshows, expos and industry groups about your group
- ✓ Notify your local business club or industry association
- ✓ Ask the members of Grow Your Business Club to share it for you

You have enough concepts, techniques, ideas and recommendations above for a year-long promotional strategy using just 1 a week. Start combining different tactics and strategies to maximise and increase awareness and exposure of your impending Facebook group launch.

Pick your top 5 favourites from the list above and execute/implement them.

Keep coming back for more ideas to promote your NEW Facebook Group.

Address the WIFM Factor Straight Away

Now we touched on this right at the start with Facebook Group Header. OK, so you've created your group description and added some rules.

Now, one of the things we touched on earlier is your call to action in the group description, and offering a FREE item of value. For me I offer one of 4 FREE items of value when people contact me or join my group on Facebook. I call them an Instant Breakthrough (IBT). I offer 4 FREE IBTs, one for each stage of the Entrepreneurial Journey.

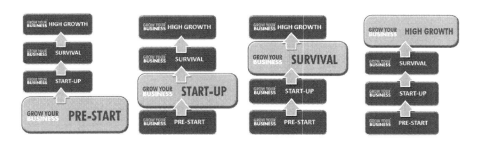

Pre-Start Entrepreneurs

If you are at a cross roads and haven't yet thought of starting a business, then download your FREE Instant Breakthrough Checklist to help you identify what's holding you back and preventing you from achieving your personal goals and objectives.

Get it for FREE at https://www.gybtv.net/experience-an-instant-breakthrough-01/.

Start-up Entrepreneurs

If you are struggling to document your model, vision or strategy or need help to identify why your marketing isn't working and which routes to market to focus on, then then download your FREE Instant Breakthrough Checklist to help you identify what's holding you back and preventing you from achieving your marketing goals and objectives.

Get it for **FREE** at https://www.gybtv.net/experience-an-instant-breakthrough-02a/

Existing Small Business Owners

If you're struggling to generate the results you want from your marketing then download your FREE Instant Breakthrough Checklist to help you identify what's holding you back and preventing you from achieving your online marketing goals and objectives.

Get it for **FREE** HERE – https://www.gybtv.net/experience-an-instant-breakthrough-03a

High Growth Business Owners

If you're struggling to generate and record the growth you want then download your FREE Instant Breakthrough Checklist to help you identify what's holding you back and preventing you from achieving the growth you want with your business.

Get it for FREE, HERE - https://www.gybtv.net/experience-an-instant-breakthrough-04a

50 Practical Things to Share in Your Group

OK, you've thought about the NLP implications of communicating with your group. You've thought about the implications of their information needs. Now what about at a practical and creative level? What the heck are you going to post about and share in your group?

Now, if you're struggling what to decide to write or post about then here's 50 ideas for posting in your group, then using just one suggestion per week from the list below, you have a year-long group posting strategy to integrate a share in your group marketing strategy.

Don't forget to ask your group members to like, comment and share your posts for bigger results.

Things to share in posts inside your group:

1. Who's done an excellent job for you - write a positive case study for them.
2. Customer CASE STUDIES - Remind readers of your successes
3. Common MISTAKES that people make, and how to avoid them

4. Daily Topical News

5. Share some interesting FACTS about your INDUSTRY

6. A relevant HUMOUROUS story to show you have a sense of humour

7. Who has really p****d you off or let you down. Share your experience.

8. Search YOUTUBE relevant topics and embed videos into your group

9. Create your own VIDEOS and upload them into your group

10. Share your own POWERPOINTS from Slideshare.net into your group

11. Debunk a Myth about your industry

12. Write about something you're PASSIONATE about

13. Embed your own .PDF documents from docstoc.com into your blog

14. Customer PAIN - Remind your readers of the problems you solve

15. Embed your own WORD documents from scribd.com into your blog

16. Share some interesting FACTS about your PRODUCTS & SERVICES

17. Share the PROBLEMS of your INDUSTRY and some potential SOLUTIONS

18. Do you have some amazing facts that you want to share with visitors?

19. Invite GUEST BLOGGERS to post relevant content into your blog

20. Is there a CAUSE or CHARITY that you care about?

21. Create a top 10 TIPS outlining some hints and tips for blog readers

22. Include a wee poll or survey in your blog

23. Share your views of the WORLD

24. Write a list of FAQs of potential objections for your services & address each one

25. Ask a question in your headline to draw people into your blog

26. Use Pingler.com or Bulkping.com to "Ping" your blog url

27. Industry TRENDS - What are the emerging markets/opportunities?

28. Include your own infographics in your blogs

29. Explain how a particular PROCESS works - Break it down for people

30. Debunk a Myth about your products and services

31. Is there a local CAUSE or COMMUNITY project that you feel strongly about?

32. If you don't have any goto google images & search for "keyword infographic"

33. Industry NEWS - What's happening in your Niche?

34. Do a software walk thru using screengrabs in your blogs using capturewizpro

35. Include a screengrab of a product in a product review

36. Share the FRUSTRATIONS of your INDUSTRY

37. Whose book have you read lately? Write a review

38. Who has really p****d you off or let you down. Share your experience.

39. Do you have some excellent market research findings you want to share?

40. Have someone interview you, and record it?

41. Why not interview someone else and record it?

42. Share an experience about a RISK you took, and the REWARD you got

43. Ask for OPINIONS on a particular topic or Issue

44. Debunk a Myth about you

45. Share some interesting FACTS about YOU

46. Share a solution to a specific, RELEVANT problem

47. Embed a PHOTO from Flickr or Photobucket (funny, strange, topical etc)

48. Embed a VIDEO testimonial

49. Write an upbeat INSPIRATIONAL post to give your readers a mental boost

50. AUDIO Record your Blog and upload to iTUNES (or similar.)

Whatever you decide, Remember:

A post could be from a SPEAKING TOPIC for your speaking engagements
A post could be a PODCAST
A post could be a VIDEO
A post could be a WEBINAR
A post could be a POWERPOINT
A post could be an article or a link to a BLOG

It could be yours. It could be a members'. It could be one of your clients, or someone you admire.

You choose, and encourage your members to post.

Nurture & Motivate

Imagine having a community online where people want to go and contribute knowing they will get your help, guidance and support.

A group should be treated like a bank account.

The more you contribute, the more the value increases, the more active you become, then the more visible and respected you become – the same is true of EVERY MEMBER IN YOUR GROUP.

The more the members contribute to it, the more the value further increases.

If people just take from the group, guess what? The value decreases.

Once again, my Group mantra in Grow Your Business Club comes into play –

"Givers gain, takers drain and lurkers simply remain the same."

Some groups on Facebook have over 150,000 members. Imaging if you had a list that big.

At the time of writing, my own group is small, it's tight and it's brand new, but every single pore in my genetic makeup is buzzing, on point and on fire, and the members are ace. Yes there are a few lurkers, and some have started sharing, connecting and posting.

We just don't know how big it's going to get ;)

I'm loving sharing, connecting and putting people together as I help people to grow their business online, and would love for you to join the evolution, be the change you want to experience online and accept my FREE invitation to join my group - Grow Your Business Club on Facebook.

One Last Thing...

Have you found **value** and **benefit** from reading this book and in being introduced to different ideas to improve your Facebook marketing by setting up your own group?

Do you think others struggling with Facebook marketing would find a **benefit** from reading this book?

Would you be prepared to **recommend** my book to others, or be prepared to write a positive review about it?

Who would be the first two people that you know who are self-employed or running their own business, that might benefit from reading this book and getting help by joining our group?

I really hope you have got value from my book. You definitely will if you choose to take action, and start making changes to your prospecting with the ideas and recommendations I've shared.

Take a moment, reflect on this book and write down the top 5 key "takeaways" you've gained from this book. Write what you've learned and consider adding a review of the book, for amazing things are about to start happening when you begin embracing and applying the principles contained herein, and when you join Grow Your Business Club.

If you're enjoying the book, consider sharing your thoughts on Facebook by uploading a wee video and sharing your thoughts. If you believe the book is worth telling others about, please would you take a few seconds to let your friends know about it? If it turns out to make a difference in their lives and businesses on Facebook, they'll be forever grateful to you, as will I.

You can add your review by revisiting our product page in the Amazon Kindle Store and upload a wee short positive video testimonial to Facebook, I'd like to say thank you in a very special way:

Managing expectation can sometimes be difficult. It can be more difficult if you don't have a plan or a system to follow on a daily basis. Inside the club, I have a very special tool to help you increase the ROI from your Facebook marketing and to help you grow your business online.

A FREE WEBINAR

It's very easy to go onto Facebook, and before you know it you've read updates, looked at pictures of cats, gone to groups, view other people's posts and a couple of hours have passed and you have nothing to show for it.

https://www.Facebook.com/fraser.hay.792/videos/10157073066873908/

With The Facebook Planner, you can save time, money and grow your business online. Would you like a FREE copy of the Planner? If so, I've got a proposition for you, if you've enjoyed my book…

MAKE ME A PROMISE & I'LL GIVE YOU A GUARANTEE

PROMISE TO…

1. **Watch the Webinar**
2. **Leave a wee positive review about my book on its Amazon page and upload a short wee positive video to Facebook.**
3. **PM me via Facebook, with a copy of the URL with your wee positive review, saying:**

"FB PLANNER PLEASE – BOOK REVIEW DONE"

AND IN RETURN, I GUARANTEE TO…

4. **Verify your review, then send you a FREE copy of The Facebook Planner, the training guide and video it's worth £49.95, but in return for doing a wee positive review, you can get your copy of the advanced Facebook Planner for FREE as a thank you from me.**

A freebie from a Scotsman? Who'd have thought? ;)

Join Grow Your Business Club

If you've read this book and enjoyed it, are ready to join the evolution and be the change you want to experience online then get help guidance and support to grow your business and sign up to the club for FREE today – Before your competitors do.

Visiting my website https://www.growyourbusiness.club

JOIN TODAY FOR FREE

About The Author

Unlike many business coaches and marketing consultants, Fraser has helped entrepreneurs from 44 countries to identify & address over 2000 common small business and entrepreneurial issues, challenges & obstacles that have been holding them back & preventing them from achieving their entrepreneurial goals & objectives.

Each of these issues have been documented and shared in his books on Amazon, webinars, keynotes, workshops and coaching programs.

He offers no prescriptive advice, but best of all - Progress is measured, documented & guaranteed.

Can he help you?

Maybe. Maybe not.

Yes, if you want to:

- Document your model, vision or strategy
- Save time & get results from your sales prospecting
- Require a fuller pipeline, sales funnel or CRM system
- Want increased awareness & exposure for your brand
- Grow Your Business®

If any of the above describe your current situation then imagine a few weeks from now, experiencing the positive, permanent breakthroughs you or your stakeholders would like.

Many individuals are just too busy dealing with the symptoms of a hectic schedule and lifestyle to identify & address the root cause of their frustrations or lack of results.

Many just need a NEW plan of action.

SOME QUICK FACTS

- 18 books published on Amazon, many reached #1 for their category
- Author of "The Lead Generation MBA" Marketing Course
- He's been featured on TV
- He has over 400 testimonials on the UKs oldest social network
- He's a former Scottish & UK Shell Livewire Winner
  He's a former Royal Bank of Scotland & Prince's Scottish Youth Business Trust winner
- Founder of Grow Your Business®
- For more facts, download his Keynote Speaker Kit on his LinkedIn profile

HE WORKS WITH

- Entrepreneurs
- Business Owners

• C Level Managers
• Board Members

of

• Pre start
• Start-up
• Small
• High Growth Businesses

He can also assist you in creating a measurable, practical plan of action via Grow Your Business® coaching or consultancy.

If required, He can also help you or your team to EXECUTE your plan.

Coaching Programs include:-

1. Personal Development & Life Coaching
2. Considering self-employment
3. How to write and execute a Social Media Marketing Plan
4. 90 Day Marketing Plan
5. Digital profits - Get your Book Published
6. How to write and execute your Business Development Plan
7. Webinar Marketing & more: Visit https://www.gybtv.net

For a FREE "Instant Breakthrough", PM him or join his group on Facebook at
https://www.Facebook.com/groups/growyourbusinessclub/ or visit
https://www.growyourbusiness.club
Whether it's coaching, consultancy, a keynote presentation or to discuss a potential JV opportunity, you can always skype him on "Pocket mentor"or call him on +44 1542 841319.

Other Work by the Author

For more, visit: www.fraserhay.com

Printed in Great Britain
by Amazon